I AM

Phoenix Rising
Unlocking the Power of Self-Acceptance

By
Gladys Martin

Copyright © 2024 by Gladys F. Martin

All rights reserved.

Published by: Book Publishing Lab

2 St Johns Ln, New York, NY 10013, USA

No portion of this book may be reproduced in any form without written permission from the publisher or author, except as permitted by U.S. copyright law.

Acknowledgement

I'm overwhelmed with gratitude for every person who's walked alongside me on this journey. Each of you brought something unique and invaluable to the creation of this book.

To my publishing team, I'm endlessly thankful. Adam Hall, Sr. Publishing & Marketing Specialist—your expertise and steady guidance have been pillars in bringing this vision to life. Luke Vale, my project manager, you managed every detail with care and patience, helping this work flourish in ways I could only have dreamed.

Rosalyn Fung, Transformational Leadership Business Coach, Spiritual Guide, and Flourishing Workplace Trainer & Facilitator—you changed my life in the most profound way. You were the first to invite me onto this path of spiritual awakening, sparking a journey that has transformed me deeply. I'm so grateful for the compassion and grace you showed me along the way.

Tina Wong, founder of True Alignment and a Channel of the Divine, thank you for your wisdom and guidance. You taught me the power of self-love and helped me believe in myself in ways I hadn't before. Your mentorship uplifted me at every step.

Elis Elizabeth, you've been a true blessing. Through your healing workshops and spiritual insight, I've experienced deep transformation and a peace I never knew was possible. I'm so grateful for every moment of growth you've inspired.

To my family—my parents, siblings, husband, and children—your love, understanding, and patience have been my foundation.

Thank you for your support through every long hour and quiet reflection. I couldn't have done this without you.

And to Coffee, my beloved puppy, whose joyful presence and boundless energy lifted my spirits on even the toughest days. You reminded me to pause, breathe, and appreciate the simple joys in life. Thank you for being my constant companion and a source of unconditional love.

This book, I Am Rising Phoenix: Unlocking the Power of Self-Acceptance, is a shared dream, shaped by all of us. Thank you for believing in me and making this journey possible.

Dedication

To my parents, Wilfredo and Henrietta, whose love, guidance, and unwavering belief in me have been my foundation. I hope this journey and these words make you as proud as I am grateful to be your child.

To my beloved husband, Chris, my steadfast partner and greatest supporter, who has shared every triumph and trial with me. Your love and encouragement fuel my courage and determination.

To my children, LJ, JC, and Ashley, who light up my life and fill my heart with purpose. You are my inspiration to live fully and with authenticity.

And to my siblings, Henri and Sheena, my lifelong friends and allies. The memories and laughter we've shared ground me and give me strength.

This book is for all of you, with love and deepest gratitude.

Table of Contents

Acknowledgement i
Dedication iii
Chapter 1 The Journey Begins 1
   Understanding Self-Acceptance 1
   Embracing Your Self; Why It Matters 2
Chapter 2 The Ashes of Self-Doubt 4
   Identifying Negative Self-Talk 4
   The Impact of Comparison on Self-Worth 5
Chapter 3 Rising from Adversity 7
   Personal Stories of Transformation 7
   Learning from Failure and Setbacks 9
Chapter 4 Cultivating Self-Love 12
   The Foundations of Self-Care 12
   Practices for Daily Self-Compassion 13
Chapter 5 The Power of Mindset 16
   Shifting Perspectives 16
   Embracing a Growth Mindset 17
Chapter 6 Building Resilience 19
   Strategies for Overcoming Challenges 19
   The Role of Support Systems 20
Chapter 7 The Art of Forgiveness 22
   Letting Go of Past Hurts 22
   My Story: Finding Forgiveness 23
   Forgiving Yourself for Mistakes 24
Chapter 8 Authenticity and Expression 26

Finding Your Voice 26

Creative Outlets for Self-Discovery 27

Chapter 9 Inspiring Others through Self-Acceptance 29

Leading by Example 29

Empowering Others in Their Journeys 30

Chapter 10 Creating a Legacy of Acceptance 32

Teaching Self-Love to Future Generations 32

Building Communities of Support and Growth 33

Book Summary 35

For my family: you are my strength and inspiration. You mean the world to me. I am grateful for your presence as I journey to transform myself into a full-grown butterfly.

Chapter 1
The Journey Begins

Understanding Self-Acceptance

Embracing self-appreciation is like granting ourselves the freedom to live truthfully and meaningfully. It begins with seeing ourselves in full, acknowledging both strengths and struggles, victories and mistakes. For young people navigating the labyrinth of self-discovery, self-appreciation serves as a shield against society's relentless demands and expectations. Embracing who they are isn't merely about forming a deep inner bond; it's also about opening up to genuine connections with others. This isn't a sudden revelation that occurs in a single moment. Instead, it's a continuous journey of learning and growth, where new insights await at every turn.

Self-care is about treating ourselves with the same kindness we'd show a friend—learning to quiet that inner critic and replace judgment with compassion. When we recognize and embrace both our strengths and our struggles, we build a solid relationship with ourselves, one that shapes how we connect with others and inspires them to embrace their own vulnerabilities. Understanding our worth means valuing what we bring to the world. Facing our past isn't about sifting through memories to pick out the "good" and "bad" ones; it's about accepting all of them—the things we tend to overlook and the moments that make us proud. Every experience, every mistake, and every success plays a role in shaping who we are. By recognizing and making peace with our experiences, we free ourselves from shame and regret, turning them into lessons that guide us forward.

This journey takes courage, especially when it means confronting parts of ourselves we'd rather hide. But in that openness, we find real strength. When we show up as our true selves, unfiltered, it creates space for genuine connection, built on mutual respect and trust. Self-esteem isn't just something that affects us alone; it radiates outward, building empathy and support in the people around us and encouraging them to face their own insecurities, right alongside us.

Embracing Your Self; Why It Matters

Embracing your true self is an act of defiance in a world that often urges us to conform. It's a journey that unlocks your potential and grounds you in who you truly are. People from all walks of life—regardless of gender, sexuality, or background—can find strength in owning their identities, and this self-acceptance often inspires others to do the same. Celebrities like Shawn Mendes, Lady Gaga, Kristen Stewart, and Angelina Jolie have publicly embraced their identities, using their platforms to empower others and advocate for inclusion. Even icons like Marlon Brando chose authenticity over expectations, showing that being yourself isn't just freeing—it's inspiring.

Self-love goes beyond a trend. It takes courage to accept yourself without constant comparison or reassurance. This freedom nurtures a powerful relationship with yourself, building resilience in difficult times. For young people wrestling with questions of identity, knowing they deserve love just as they are can be life-changing. Self-acceptance also brings real benefits to well-being: reduced anxiety, better self-esteem, and a strengthened ability to cope with challenges.

When we're open about our struggles, we inspire those around us to face theirs, fostering a shared spirit of self-acceptance. The journey of self-love is continuous, demanding both effort and patience. Yet by prioritizing it, you not only enrich your own life but also contribute to a broader cultural shift that values authenticity. As each of us embraces who we truly are, we help create a world where our diversity becomes a source of positive change. Embrace yourself, and watch how everything around you begins to transform.

Chapter 2
The Ashes of Self-Doubt

Identifying Negative Self-Talk

Learning to understand and manage our inner dialogue is essential to building self-love and personal growth, no matter our age or background. So many of us struggle with an inner voice that chips away at our self-esteem through harsh criticisms and constant self-doubt. This kind of mindset can make it hard to recognize and appreciate our own worth. But by noticing these patterns and gently replacing them with compassion, we can change how we see ourselves.

Teens and young people often feel intense self-doubt, fueled by pressures from social media, school, and peers. Thoughts like "Am I good enough?" and "Do I fit in?" can overshadow each person's unique qualities. Guiding young people to see these doubts as insecurities—rather than truths—can be a powerful step toward self-awareness. By identifying where these doubts come from, whether outside influences or internal worries, individuals can start to reclaim control over their own story.

Adults, too, face these struggles, especially parents whose responsibilities and aspirations sometimes intensify feelings of inadequacy. Questions like "Why didn't I manage to do it all?" or "Am I letting my family down?" can easily trigger cycles of guilt and frustration. But remembering that our worth isn't tied to accomplishments or others' opinions is key. By challenging these beliefs, adults can foster an environment of self-awareness and resilience for themselves and those they care about.

The journey to understanding and managing our inner dialogue takes patience and dedication. But by transforming our thoughts into positive affirmations rooted in self-love and respect, we can uplift not only ourselves but also those around us. Embracing both our strengths and imperfections allows us to grow, inspiring others to help create a community based on empowerment and acceptance.

The Impact of Comparison on Self-Worth

In a world where success seems to be on display everywhere, it's hard not to compare ourselves to others—especially for young people scrolling through idealized lives on social media. These carefully curated images can overshadow the struggles that everyone faces, leaving us feeling like we don't measure up. But realizing that each person's journey is different can empower us to embrace our own path. Rather than falling into the trap of constant comparison, we can learn to appreciate our individuality and celebrate even the smallest wins along the way.

Our sense of self-worth is closely tied to the stories we tell ourselves. When we focus on how we compare to others or seek approval outside ourselves, we can easily undermine our confidence. To break free from this pattern, we need to redirect our attention inward and nurture self-appreciation. Acknowledging our abilities and accomplishments—even the small ones—builds a solid foundation of self-worth that stays steady, no matter what others think.

As we get to know ourselves better, it's also important to connect with supportive people. Having mentors, friends, and guides who value our unique qualities reminds us that everyone's path is one of a kind. These relationships help reinforce that our worth doesn't depend on comparisons but on the richness of our own experiences.

In this kind of supportive space, we learn to appreciate ourselves and others, creating a community based on encouragement instead of competition.

At the end of the day, we all struggle with the impact of comparisons on our self-esteem. By choosing to avoid constant comparison, we can start to truly value our own journey and, in doing so, inspire others to do the same. Let's focus on accepting and supporting ourselves, knowing that our strength comes from lifting each other up. When we recognize the power within us and shift from comparison to embracing our growth, we create room for real self-appreciation to flourish, even in challenging times.

Chapter 3
Rising from Adversity

Personal Stories of Transformation

Embarking on a journey of self-exploration often starts with hearing stories of growth that offer guidance and inspiration. Each story reveals resilience in the face of challenges and the journey of discovering one's identity. These firsthand accounts resonate with people of all ages, offering encouragement just when it's needed most. In hard times, these stories remind us of our own strength and potential. By embracing vulnerability, we uncover lessons within our hardships, experiencing firsthand how they can foster growth and self-belief.

For much of my life, I struggled with self-doubt, feeling like I didn't measure up to my peers or deserve love the way they did. I constantly questioned my worth, feeling like an outsider in my own life. Then, one day, I met a mentor who began to change everything. This mentor taught me the importance of being kind to myself and how positive affirmations could shift my mindset. Little by little, I began challenging the negative thoughts that once held me back, replacing them with affirmations that celebrated what made me unique. I began to embrace my individuality, focusing on my strengths rather than my perceived flaws.

Over time, I experienced a profound transformation. I went from struggling with self-doubt to genuinely loving who I am, accepting all the unique qualities and imperfections that make me who I am. This journey wasn't easy, but it was worth every step. Today, I feel empowered by my story and grateful for the strength I discovered within.

Then there's Mark, a father who wrestled with society's expectations of masculinity. For years, he felt boxed in by a rigid mold that dictated how he "should" express emotions. After attending a workshop on emotional intelligence, he realized how powerful vulnerability could be in building genuine connections with his children. Mark began sharing his feelings openly, showing his kids that not only is it okay to feel, but it's also essential to embrace those feelings. His journey of self-acceptance transformed him and brought him closer to his family, teaching them the value of emotional honesty and resilience.

Stories like these remind us that transformation often requires facing our fears and insecurities. For many, it means stepping out of familiar comfort zones and challenging beliefs they've held for years. By sharing personal experiences, we inspire one another to explore our own paths, showing that each of us has the strength to rise from struggles—like a phoenix from the ashes.

Ultimately, personal stories of transformation show us that self-acceptance is a journey, not a destination. By sharing and celebrating these journeys, we create a supportive community where each story has the potential to spark change—not only for the people telling them but also for those who listen and learn. Embracing our paths and the paths of others unlocks the power of self-love, spreading empowerment that can ripple through generations. Together, we can rise, transform, and inspire each other to embrace the beauty of our true selves.

Learning from Failure and Setbacks

Failures and setbacks can feel like roadblocks, but they're often our greatest opportunities for growth and self-discovery. When challenges hit, we usually feel disappointed or frustrated at first. But if we can shift our perspective, we start to see these moments as valuable lessons that move us forward. Embracing failure doesn't mean we're weak; it shows resilience and a real commitment to becoming our best selves. Every setback gives us a chance to look closely at our goals, values, and motivations, bringing us closer to who we really are.

Take my journey as an entrepreneur, for example. I've faced countless hurdles, especially while building my first construction company. Managing client expectations was tough, and later, when my team and I set out to create the first Filipino-Canadian-themed RV park and campground in North America, we encountered even more obstacles. We poured our hearts into this project for five years, often losing bids on properties we'd hoped would be part of our vision. Some days, we were completely drained, questioning if it was all worth it.

Then, there's the journey of advocating for mental health—something I'm passionate about, but that's often met with resistance or indifference. Raising awareness and encouraging people to support those dealing with mental health issues hasn't been easy; at times, it's felt like shouting into the void. It can be incredibly disheartening when people ignore or shy away from these conversations, especially when you see how much of a difference support can make for someone who's struggling. But over time, I've come to realize that every small effort counts. Every conversation, every piece of support offered to someone in need, makes a difference. And through this work, I've found a deeper resilience, realizing that even when I feel alone, these efforts can spark change.

Despite the setbacks, I stayed committed. Each challenge, whether in business or in advocacy, taught me resilience and made me more determined. I've learned that obstacles, as hard as they are, can help us grow stronger and bring us closer to our dreams.

As we go through life, it's easy to let the fear of failure hold us back, keeping us from taking risks and following what truly matters to us. Yet it's often in our hardest moments that we discover our greatest strengths. People who've faced big challenges often come out of them stronger, proving that failure isn't the end—it's a stepping stone. When we allow ourselves to be vulnerable and open to what these experiences can teach us, we create a mindset that welcomes growth. This shift empowers us to rise from failure, much like a phoenix from the ashes.

As we navigate life's ups and downs, self-compassion is essential. Instead of judging ourselves harshly when we fall short, we can approach ourselves with kindness and understanding. This gentler approach helps us process what we're feeling and move forward with renewed purpose. Recognizing that setbacks are part of everyone's journey also connects us to each other, building a culture of self-acceptance and support that lifts us all up.

Learning from failure is a transformative experience that opens the door to personal growth. Each time we overcome a challenge, we become more self-aware, more resilient, and unlock more of our potential. By embracing our failures and using them as stepping stones, we don't just empower ourselves—we inspire others. The journey of self-love and acceptance is ongoing, and each setback is a chance to rise stronger, wiser, and more true to ourselves. In this way, failure becomes not a barrier, but a powerful teacher, guiding us toward a brighter, more authentic future.

Chapter 4
Cultivating Self-Love

The Foundations of Self-Care

Self-care isn't just a trend; it's a foundation for living a meaningful, fulfilling life. At its heart, self-care is about knowing your own worth and making your well-being a priority. This journey begins with self-acceptance—acknowledging that you deserve kindness and compassion. When you embrace who you are, flaws and all, you create fertile ground for growth and resilience. Each small act of self-care is a declaration of your value, a way of honoring your unique path and the struggles you've overcome.

Building a solid foundation of self-care starts with self-awareness. This means taking time to understand your thoughts, emotions, and behaviors. Recognizing what triggers you and understanding your needs gives you the power to make choices that truly nourish your spirit. For young people trying to find their way with identity and self-image, building this awareness can be a game changer. It lets you quiet the inner critic and nurture a supportive voice that celebrates what makes you unique.

Another essential piece of self-care is learning to set boundaries. Being able to say "no" without guilt is a powerful act of self-respect. Boundaries protect your energy and mental well-being, allowing you to focus on relationships and activities that lift you up rather than drain you. Healthy boundaries show others that it's okay to put yourself first sometimes while still being kind and compassionate. This balance creates a culture of respect and self-worth that radiates into families, friendships, and communities.

Incorporating mindfulness into your self-care routine can change how you experience life's daily moments. Mindfulness invites you to be present, to find beauty in small things, and to meet your feelings without judgment. Whether through meditation, journaling, or simply taking a deep breath, mindfulness helps you reconnect with yourself. For many, this reconnection brings a new sense of strength and empowerment, the realization that you can shape your reality and meet challenges with grace.

Finally, self-care also means celebrating your achievements, both big and small. Recognizing your progress strengthens your confidence and reinforces a positive self-image. For teachers and coaches, celebrating the efforts of students and athletes creates an environment where everyone feels valued. This isn't just about celebrating success; it's about honoring the courage to try, the resilience to keep going, and the willingness to learn and grow.

Every step you take toward self-love is a step toward empowerment. When you rise from your struggles, you don't just lift yourself up—you also inspire others to begin their own journeys of self-discovery and acceptance. In the end, self-care is a way of saying, "I matter." And that's a message we all deserve to live by.

Practices for Daily Self-Compassion

Daily self-compassion is essential for nurturing a resilient spirit and embracing our true selves. It begins with the simple yet profound act of treating ourselves with the same kindness and understanding we would offer a close friend. When faced with challenges or setbacks, we are often quick to judge ourselves harshly. Instead, we can acknowledge our feelings without criticism, recognizing that imperfection is part of the human experience. By cultivating this mindset, we create a safe space for growth and healing, allowing ourselves to rise from the ashes of self-doubt and disappointment.

One powerful practice for fostering self-compassion is using positive affirmations. Each day, take a moment to speak kindly to yourself, reinforcing the belief that you are worthy of love and acceptance. Start with simple statements like "I am enough" or "I embrace my journey." Writing these affirmations down and placing them in visible spots serves as a gentle reminder of your inherent value. Over time, these affirmations can transform negative self-talk into a nurturing inner dialogue, empowering you to face life's challenges with grace and resilience.

Mindfulness is another effective way to practice self-compassion. Being present in the moment allows us to observe our thoughts and feelings without judgment. This practice encourages us to acknowledge our struggles while recognizing that we are not alone in our experiences. Engaging in mindful breathing or meditation can ground us, fostering a sense of calm and acceptance. As we cultivate this awareness, we learn to treat ourselves with gentleness, opening our hearts to the possibility of healing and self-love.

Journaling is a transformative tool for self-reflection and compassion. Putting pen to paper allows us to explore our emotions and experiences in a safe, private space. Begin by writing about moments when you felt inadequate or faced criticism. Then, challenge those negative thoughts by reframing them with compassion. Ask yourself what you would say to a friend in a similar situation. This practice helps us process our feelings and reinforces the idea that we can be our own best allies, rising above self-judgment and shame.

Finally, surrounding ourselves with supportive individuals can greatly enhance our journey toward self-compassion. Seek out friends or communities that celebrate authenticity and vulnerability. Engage in conversations that uplift and inspire, and share your experiences with those who understand the power of self-acceptance. By fostering connections with others who champion compassion, we create a network of support that empowers us to become more resilient, deeply in love with ourselves, and ready for a brighter future.

Chapter 5
The Power of Mindset

Shifting Perspectives

Shifting perspectives is more than just a mental exercise—it's a journey that lets us reexamine the stories we tell about ourselves and the world around us. These stories shape our reality, and by learning to shift how we see things, we open the door to self-acceptance and genuine empowerment. This kind of change starts with recognizing that we aren't defined by past mistakes or other people's judgments. Instead, we're shaped by our choices, our resilience, and our capacity to grow. Taking on a fresh viewpoint helps us move past self-doubt and limitations, allowing our truest selves to emerge.

When facing adversity, shifting perspectives becomes a tool we can lean on. Challenges may feel overwhelming, but if we look at them as chances to grow, everything starts to shift. Every obstacle is an opportunity to learn more about who we are and build resilience. By choosing to see difficulties as stepping stones instead of setbacks, we give ourselves control over our narrative. This shift not only builds self-love but also inspires those around us to face their own journeys with courage and optimism.

Self-love and shifting perspectives are deeply connected. Accepting ourselves—flaws and all—creates a foundation for genuine personal growth. This acceptance isn't about complacency; it's about understanding our worth and potential, even with all of life's messiness. When we focus on our strengths and accomplishments, we start building a positive self-image. With this newfound appreciation, we can rise above negative self-talk and societal pressures, allowing us to go after our passions without apology.

Ultimately, embracing a shift in perspective is crucial for true self-acceptance. It reminds us that each of us has the ability to rise, renew, and transform. By adopting a compassionate and open-minded outlook, we create a ripple effect of empowerment that can touch lives. Together, we foster a community where self-love grows and each person is inspired to be their authentic self. Let's celebrate the strength that comes from shifting perspectives, because in this journey, we truly rise from the ashes.

Embracing a Growth Mindset

Embracing a growth mindset sparks the fire of self-acceptance and empowers us to overcome challenges. This mindset encourages us to view obstacles as opportunities for growth, rather than immovable walls. When we adopt a growth mindset, we start to see our potential as boundless, understanding that our abilities aren't fixed but can grow with dedication and hard work. This way of thinking builds resilience and fuels a belief in constant self-improvement.

For many, self-acceptance starts with seeing failure not as an end, but as a stepping stone on the path to success. Each setback holds valuable lessons that guide us closer to our goals. By reframing failure, we empower ourselves to take risks and pursue passions without fearing judgment. Practicing self-love is essential to this mindset, because unconditional acceptance makes us more open to change and growth. Acknowledging both our strengths and weaknesses reinforces that growth is an ongoing journey.

A growth mindset also thrives in a supportive community. Surrounding ourselves with people who inspire and challenge us can make all the difference. Meaningful conversations about growth, resilience, and self-acceptance encourage us to share our stories and learn from each other. Together, we create an atmosphere where everyone feels valued and uplifted, allowing us to rise together.

Ultimately, embracing a growth mindset changes how we speak to ourselves and reshapes our story. It encourages us to be proactive about our growth and to approach life with an open heart and mind. This shift—at any age—is a powerful tool that opens doors to self-discovery and acceptance. When we believe in our potential and support each other, we can rise from the ashes of self-doubt, emerging stronger, more empowered, and ready to embrace the fullness of life

Chapter 6
Building Resilience

Strategies for Overcoming Challenges

Embracing self-acceptance is a journey filled with challenges, yet each obstacle can become a stepping-stone toward empowerment. One effective strategy for overcoming these challenges is to cultivate a growth mindset, which encourages viewing difficulties not as barriers but as opportunities for learning and growth. By reframing setbacks as valuable lessons, we foster resilience and gain a deeper understanding of ourselves. When faced with adversity, remind yourself that every experience shapes you into a stronger, more self-aware individual.

Building a supportive community is also essential. Surround yourself with positive influences who uplift you. Engage in open conversations, share your struggles, and seek encouragement from those who inspire. A solid support system provides emotional backing and diverse perspectives to help navigate challenging times. Remember, you are not alone; there are people who understand and are willing to walk alongside you.

Practicing self-compassion is vital in overcoming challenges. Often, we are our harshest critics, and negative self-talk can hinder our ability to accept and love ourselves. Instead of focusing on perceived flaws, approach yourself with kindness and understanding. Treat yourself as you would a dear friend. Acknowledging that imperfection is part of being human fosters a sense of peace and acceptance that propels you forward.

Setting realistic goals can further aid in overcoming challenges. Breaking down aspirations into manageable steps creates a sense of accomplishment at each stage, making daunting tasks feel achievable and reinforcing positive self-affirmation. Celebrate your progress, no matter how small, as each step contributes to your journey of self-acceptance. Recognizing your achievements builds confidence and resilience, creating momentum that drives you toward empowerment.

Finally, practicing mindfulness is a transformative strategy. By staying present and focusing on the here and now, you can reduce anxiety and self-doubt. Mindfulness encourages awareness of your thoughts and feelings without judgment, creating space for acceptance. Incorporating practices such as meditation, deep breathing, or journaling into your routine can help ground you and reinforce your commitment to self-love. Rising from adversity, these strategies empower you to embrace your true self and unlock your potential.

The Role of Support Systems

Support systems play a pivotal role in the journey of self-acceptance and empowerment. For those navigating the complexities of identity and self-worth, the presence of a supportive network can be transformative. This network—comprising friends, family, and community members—offers a safe space to express one's true self without fear of judgment. Feeling supported encourages individuals to embrace their unique qualities, cultivate self-love, and overcome challenges.

Supportive relationships provide guidance and encouragement, helping individuals recognize their strengths and navigate obstacles with confidence. By sharing insights and experiences, these relationships inspire self-acceptance and resilience, teaching that setbacks are not failures but opportunities for growth. Supportive connections instill a belief that everyone has the potential to rise, regardless of past challenges.

A culture of open dialogue about feelings and experiences creates an environment where individuals feel valued and understood. This nurturing space allows people to explore their identities and develop a sense of belonging. Modeling self-love and acceptance empowers others to embrace their individuality and confidently pursue their passions.

Ultimately, the collective power of support systems illuminates the path toward self-love and empowerment. Individuals uplift one another, creating a ripple effect that extends beyond personal journeys. Each encouragement and affirmation contributes to a greater movement of acceptance and resilience. By embracing the role of support systems, we foster a culture where self-acceptance and resilience are celebrated, unlocking the profound potential that lies within us all.

Chapter 7
The Art of Forgiveness

Letting Go of Past Hurts

Letting go of past hurts is a powerful journey that helps us unlock our fullest potential. So many of us carry the weight of old wounds, allowing them to shape our present and cast shadows on our future. But it's essential to remember that, while painful, these experiences don't define who we are. Instead of holding on to hurt, we can rise above it—like a phoenix from the ashes. This process doesn't mean forgetting; it's about reframing our story and reclaiming our power.

Embracing self-love is a key part of letting go. It means acknowledging our pain and validating our feelings without judgment. Each scar tells a story of resilience, and by honoring these stories, we build a foundation for healing. As we nurture self-compassion, we start treating ourselves with the kindness we truly deserve. This shift helps us see our past not as a source of shame but as a stepping-stone for growth, allowing us to let go of burdens we've carried for far too long.

Forgiveness is essential in letting go. It's often misunderstood as accepting what someone did to us, but in reality, forgiveness is a gift we give to ourselves. It frees us from resentment and anger—the heavy baggage we don't need. Choosing to forgive lifts the emotional weight of the past, letting us reclaim our energy and focus on the future. Forgiving doesn't mean forgetting; it means regaining the strength to move forward with grace and purpose.

Having a supportive community around us can also make a big difference in our healing journey. Being surrounded by people who lift us up creates a safe space where we can heal. Sharing our experiences with friends, family, or support groups lightens our emotional load and reminds us we're not alone. In these spaces, we find comfort and inspiration to move on from the past and look toward a brighter future.

Healing is a process, not a destination. Each step brings us closer to self-acceptance and empowerment. Embracing our vulnerabilities makes us stronger—like the phoenix that symbolizes renewal. Letting go of past hurts creates space for new experiences and relationships, inviting us to step into our true selves and soar to new heights.

My Story: Finding Forgiveness

In my own journey, I faced the pain of betrayal by people I once considered family. Friends I trusted and treated like my own turned out to be speaking about me behind my back, casting doubt on our bond and leaving me with a profound sense of hurt. At first, letting go of the resentment felt impossible as I struggled with disbelief and anger. But I came to realize that holding on to this pain only kept me chained to the past, allowing the betrayal to keep influencing my life.

Forgiving them didn't mean forgetting their actions or inviting them back into my life. Instead, I chose to release the anger and reclaim my peace. By forgiving, I freed myself from their hold on my thoughts and emotions. This act of forgiveness let me move forward without the weight of the past. It wasn't easy, but each day I reminded myself that I deserved to live unburdened by others' actions. By letting go, I embraced a renewed sense of self—stronger and more compassionate than before.

Forgiving Yourself for Mistakes

Forgiving yourself for mistakes is one of the most powerful acts of self-love. Many of us carry the weight of past actions like a heavy backpack, constantly reminding ourselves of what we "should have" done differently. But it's essential to remember that mistakes are just part of being human. Instead of letting guilt and shame hold you back, see these moments as chances to grow. Each misstep teaches us something valuable, helping us build resilience and a deeper understanding of ourselves.

On the path to self-acceptance, embracing your imperfections is crucial. Acknowledge that mistakes don't define you; doing so creates space for compassion and understanding. Treat yourself with the same kindness you'd offer a friend facing similar struggles. When you stumble, encourage yourself instead of criticizing. This simple shift changes how you see your past, allowing you to rise from the ashes of regret and step into the light of new possibilities.

Self-forgiveness starts with reflection. Take time to look at the choices you made and what influenced them. Were fear, pressure, or inexperience part of the picture? Understanding the context helps you see that you did the best you could at that moment. This isn't about making excuses; it's about embracing your humanity. By recognizing the factors behind your mistakes, you cultivate empathy for yourself, paving the way for healing.

Letting go of perfectionism is also key to forgiving yourself. Perfectionism can trap us in cycles of self-judgment and disappointment. Give yourself permission to be imperfect. Celebrate small victories along the way, and remember that growth takes time. Each step toward self-forgiveness is proof of your strength and resilience. Letting go of past mistakes is liberating; it's an affirmation of your worthiness and potential.

Ultimately, forgiving yourself is a powerful choice. It shows your commitment to becoming the best version of yourself, unburdened by past errors. Embracing self-forgiveness opens up new possibilities, making you more resilient, compassionate, and aligned with your true self. Rising from the ashes of your past, remember that each day is a new chance to reshape your story. Let your journey of self-acceptance inspire not just you but also those around you, creating a ripple effect of empowerment and love.

Chapter 8
Authenticity and Expression

Finding Your Voice

Finding your voice is a transformative journey that begins with self-discovery and acceptance. For many, the quest to express their true selves can feel daunting, especially in a world that often imposes expectations and standards. Yet understanding that your voice matters is the first step toward empowerment. Your voice—your unique expression of thoughts, feelings, and experiences—has the power to inspire both you and those around you. This journey encourages peeling back layers of doubt and fear to embrace your authenticity.

Every individual possesses a distinct narrative shaped by personal experiences. To find your voice, begin by reflecting on your story: What challenges have you faced? What victories have you celebrated? By acknowledging the lessons from both triumphs and struggles, you build a foundation of self-love. This self-awareness fosters confidence, allowing you to articulate your thoughts and feelings with clarity and conviction. Remember, we create connections by sharing our stories and building supportive communities.

In a society that often prioritizes conformity, cultivating an environment that encourages open expression is essential. When we foster a culture of acceptance, listening, and validation, we empower individuals to explore their identities and speak their truths. Create spaces where voices are heard, celebrated, and nurtured, cultivating resilience and self-acceptance along the way.

Finding your voice also means embracing self-advocacy. It involves recognizing your worth and standing up for your beliefs, even when faced with opposition. This empowerment comes from knowing your opinions and feelings are valid. Equip yourself with tools like journaling, creative expression, or public speaking to strengthen your communication skills. Each step toward voicing your truth brings you closer to who you're meant to be, inspiring others to begin their journeys of self-discovery.

Ultimately, the path to finding your voice is an ongoing process of growth and exploration. Embrace the ups and downs, as they are integral to your evolution. As you rise from self-doubt, let your unique voice shine. Celebrate the moments when you step into your power and inspire others to do the same. Your voice has the potential to spark change, uplift others, and contribute to a more compassionate world. In this journey of self-acceptance, your voice is not just a means of expression—it is a powerful tool for transformation for both yourself and those around you.

Creative Outlets for Self-Discovery

Creative outlets serve as powerful tools for self-discovery, allowing individuals to explore their innermost thoughts and feelings. Engaging in creative activities—whether through writing, painting, music, or dance—provides a form of self-expression that transcends words. During moments of creation, one can tap into the authentic self, revealing layers of identity that may have been suppressed or overlooked. Creativity becomes a mirror, reflecting the complexities of personal experiences and emotions, enabling a deeper understanding of oneself.

Creative pursuits can be particularly transformative during adolescence, a period marked by exploration and identity formation.

Young people can channel their experiences and feelings into something tangible through journaling, crafting, or participating in theater. This expression fosters self-confidence and cultivates resilience as they navigate the challenges of growing up. Embracing creativity teaches them that their voices matter and that their stories deserve to be told.

For people of all ages, creativity offers empowerment and healing. Artistic endeavors provide a way to process both joyful and challenging life experiences. Painting a canvas or composing a song can become a cathartic release of pent-up emotions. Immersed in the creative process, many discover newfound strengths and passions that contribute to a more fulfilling life. This journey of exploration reinforces that self-acceptance is not a destination but an ongoing process enriched by creativity.

Supporting creative expression in ourselves and others can ignite a passion that fuels self-discovery. Providing resources—such as access to art supplies, music lessons, or writing workshops—empowers people to explore their creativity without fear of judgment. This support nurtures a sense of community and belonging, reminding individuals that they are not alone in their journey toward self-acceptance and empowerment.

Ultimately, embracing creative outlets is a vital step in self-discovery. In a world that often emphasizes conformity, creativity invites authenticity and individuality. As individuals rise from their challenges, they can harness the power of artistic expression to illuminate their paths. By recognizing the importance of creativity, they cultivate a deeper understanding of themselves and a greater appreciation for their unique journeys. Creative outlets become not only a means of expression but also a vital component of personal growth and self-love.

Chapter 9
Inspiring Others through Self-Acceptance

Leading by Example

Leading by example is one of the most powerful tools on the journey toward self-acceptance and empowerment. When we embody the principles we want to instill in others, we create a ripple effect that inspires change. Witnessing authentic self-love in action shows that self-acceptance is not just a concept but a way of life. Leading by example involves demonstrating vulnerability and resilience, showing that it's okay to struggle and rise again. This approach fosters a culture of acceptance, encouraging others to embrace their true selves.

Leading by example also means modeling healthy self-esteem and self-care practices. By prioritizing well-being and self-acceptance, we create a nurturing environment where self-love can flourish, empowering others to embrace their unique identities. Sharing both challenges and triumphs demystifies the path to self-acceptance, instilling a sense of hope and possibility.

In various settings, leading by example can help build supportive, inclusive communities. Demonstrating respect for oneself and others lays the foundation for a culture that celebrates individual strengths and encourages self-expression. Personal stories of growth and self-discovery can inspire others to pursue their journeys with courage and determination, reinforcing the idea that everyone, regardless of past struggles, can rise and reclaim their power.

Ultimately, leading by example is about living authentically and unapologetically. Each act of courage, each moment of vulnerability, and every expression of self-love contributes to collective empowerment that transcends individual struggles. Together, we can forge a community where self-acceptance thrives, inspiring each other to rise stronger, bolder, and more empowered.

Empowering Others in Their Journeys

Empowering others on their journeys is a transformative act that uplifts those around us and deepens our own sense of purpose and connection. In a world where challenges often feel insurmountable, offering support can ignite the flames of self-acceptance and resilience. Each person carries a unique story filled with struggles and triumphs. By honoring these narratives, we create a safe space where individuals can explore their identities, dreams, and fears. This acknowledgment is the first step toward empowerment, as it validates experiences and encourages individuals to embrace their true selves.

Empowerment also involves active listening and understanding. By genuinely hearing others, we validate their feelings and experiences, allowing them to express themselves without fear of judgment. This simple act can be transformative, encouraging deeper self-acceptance. Listening with empathy provides support and empowers others to discover their strengths. It reminds them that they possess the inner resources necessary for growth.

Encouraging self-discovery is another crucial aspect of empowerment. By asking insightful questions and guiding reflection, we help individuals uncover their passions, values, and aspirations. This fosters a sense of agency, enabling them to take charge of their lives. In a society that often imposes limitations, reminding others of their boundless potential is vital. Celebrating achievements, no matter how small, reinforces self-belief and instills pride. Recognizing one's worth and capabilities empowers individuals to pursue their dreams and advocate for themselves.

Empowering others creates a ripple effect that extends far beyond our immediate circles. As individuals grow in self-acceptance and confidence, they inspire and uplift those around them. This cycle of empowerment fosters a culture of love, support, and resilience, enabling communities to rise together. In nurturing self-acceptance in others, we contribute to a future where everyone feels valued, capable, and ready to embrace their unique journeys, witnessing their transformations and actively participating in the collective rise of the human spirit.

Chapter 10
Creating a Legacy of Acceptance

Teaching Self-Love to Future Generations

Teaching self-love to future generations is about more than just shaping individuals—it's about transforming lives and strengthening communities. In today's complex world, helping young people find self-acceptance empowers them to rise above challenges and embrace their unique selves. Self-love isn't just a buzzword; it's the foundation that pushes each of us to pursue our dreams without apology.

Leading by example is at the heart of teaching self-love. It begins with sharing our own journeys, including the times we've struggled and the moments we've triumphed. By showing vulnerability and honesty, we connect with young people and remind them that they're not alone in feeling doubt or insecurity. When we open up about our path to self-acceptance, we show that self-love is a journey, not a one-time achievement.

Creating a culture of self-love also means building emotional intelligence. Teaching young people to recognize and express their feelings allows them to better understand themselves. Activities like journaling and open discussions encourage them to talk about self-worth and their personal experiences. By giving them tools to face negative self-talk and replace it with affirmations of their strengths, we're equipping them to confront challenges with confidence.

Celebrating individuality is equally important. Each person brings something unique to the world, and recognizing this diversity helps push back against pressures to conform. When we encourage young people to explore their interests, talents, and passions, we ignite a sense of purpose and belonging. By honoring each person's unique contributions, we reinforce the idea that everyone is worthy of love and respect, just as they are.

Lastly, resilience is a key part of teaching self-love. Life will always have ups and downs, and learning to bounce back is essential. Encouraging a growth mindset helps young people see that failure isn't a reflection of their worth but an opportunity to learn and grow. Resilience reminds them that self-love is a source of strength they can lean on through life's challenges. By nurturing this mindset, we inspire a future generation that is stronger, braver, and ready to create a brighter future for themselves and those around them.

Building Communities of Support and Growth

Building communities of support and growth is essential for creating spaces where people can thrive as their true selves. In a world filled with challenges and pressures to fit in, these supportive spaces offer a spark of self-acceptance. When we gather as a community, we can share our stories, celebrate what makes each of us different, and learn from one another. This sense of belonging helps each person turn struggles into opportunities and discover their own potential.

Supportive communities provide the ground where self-love can grow. When people come together, they create networks of encouragement that remind each of us of our worth. Leaders in these communities foster open dialogue and share experiences, inspiring others to shed self-doubt and embrace who they really are. In this safe space, everyone is encouraged to challenge negative messages from society and let their unique qualities shine.

Sharing vulnerabilities within a community also deepens our connections. When people open up about their fears and insecurities, it fosters empathy and understanding. This kind of bond reminds us that none of us are alone in our struggles. Through shared stories, the wisdom of the community shines through, offering insights and support for overcoming obstacles. This shared experience builds mutual growth and strengthens the support we give one another.

A culture of recognition and celebration further enhances a community's growth. Acknowledging each other's achievements, no matter how small, creates pride and motivation. Celebrating progress and resilience shows that every step toward self-acceptance is meaningful. By highlighting growth, communities encourage a positive mindset, inspiring everyone to keep striving for self-love.

Ultimately, building communities of support and growth is essential for fostering self-acceptance and empowerment. Together, we create a powerful force that uplifts individuals and turns pain into purpose. Each person's journey is unique, but in a supportive community, these journeys intertwine, creating a tapestry of strength and resilience. By embracing our shared humanity, we lift each other out of self-doubt and light the way for ourselves and future generations. Let us commit to nurturing these communities, ensuring that everyone can flourish in a space filled with love, acceptance, and growth.

Book Summary

I Am Phoenix Rising: Unlocking the Power of Self-Acceptance is a transformative guide focused on embracing self-worth and cultivating inner strength. The book takes readers on a journey of self-discovery, emphasizing the importance of self-acceptance as a foundation for personal growth and empowerment. Through powerful narratives, reflective exercises, and actionable advice, it encourages readers to confront insecurities, break free from limiting beliefs, and embrace their authentic selves.

The concept of "rising like a phoenix" symbolizes resilience, renewal, and the courage to rise above challenges. By addressing the obstacles that often hinder self-love and self-worth, the book empowers readers to overcome past hurts and societal expectations, enabling them to live unapologetically and pursue their true passions. It highlights the importance of supportive communities, self-compassion, and mental resilience, helping readers develop tools to navigate life's ups and downs with confidence and grace.

Ultimately, I Am Phoenix Rising serves as a motivational roadmap to finding inner peace and purpose, fostering a mindset of acceptance, growth, and self-empowerment.

www.ingramcontent.com/pod-product-compliance
Ingram Content Group UK Ltd.
Pitfield, Milton Keynes, MK11 3LW, UK
UKHW050419070425
457075UK00025B/49